Shadows & Ink

Vol. 3

The Psychology of Horror Fiction

JOE MYNHARDT

Published by Crystal Lake Publishing
Where Stories Come Alive!

www.crystallakepub.com

WELCOME
TO ANOTHER

CRYSTAL LAKE PUBLISHING
CREATION

Contents

Introduction

Why do we seek out fear? It's a question that's puzzled many, myself included—even from, what I can recall, the tender age of eight. Why, in the comfort of our everyday lives, do we willingly expose ourselves to stories that unsettle, disturb, and even terrify us?

Before we dive deep into this question, here's an explanation we've all probably heard quite a few times: The appeal of horror fiction lies in its unique ability to tap into our most primal emotions, offering an experience that simultaneously repels and fascinates. From haunted houses and shadowy figures to monsters lurking in the dark, horror fiction allows us to confront our fears in a controlled, safe environment. For me personally, it's just so damn cool and fun.

But it's more than that. More than just a thrill.

Horror serves a deeper psychological purpose: it forces us to confront the unknown, grapple with existential fears, and explore the darkest corners of the human psyche. Best of all, it's a great way to make friends with similar-minded readers.

Horror fiction can be many things—gory and grotesque, subtle and suspenseful, supernatural or psychological. But at its core, horror is about the evocation of fear, tension, and the unsettling. It captivates us because it speaks to our deepest anxieties, pulling back the veil on what we normally suppress. Whether it's the creeping dread of isolation or the terror of facing the incomprehensible, horror taps into universal human experiences and emotions. In this book, we will explore not just what horror is, but why it has the power to captivate and haunt us, long after the final page is turned.

This journey will take us deep into the psychological and emotional reasons behind our fascination with fear. We'll examine how horror works on a psychological level, what draws us to it, and how writers can harness these instincts to craft stories that linger in the minds of their readers. Welcome to *The Psychology of Horror Fiction*—where we unravel the mysteries of why we love to be scared.

Who am I?

I'm Joe Mynhardt, a Bram Stoker Award-winning editor, publisher, and author with (at this moment in time) almost two decades of experience in horror fiction. As the founder and CEO of Crystal Lake Publishing, I've had the privilege of working with some of the most celebrated names in the horror world and beyond, from authors and artists to actors, puppeteers, and the Hollywood directors who made some of my favorite childhood movies—movies I snuck out of bed for late at night.

My journey into horror, and how to market it, has given me deep insight into why the genre speaks so powerfully to readers, and it's my passion to help writers understand this connection and tap into it. Through my Shadows & Ink series and my work mentoring authors, I've seen how deeply horror resonates—both for those who create it and those who consume it.

Join me as we dive into the psychology behind horror and uncover the forces that drive our fascination with the dark and terrifying.

Chapter 1
Why We Love Horror

Horror fiction has a strange allure. While the stories can terrify us and make our skin crawl, they also captivate us, drawing us back into the darkness again and again. But why do we love being scared? From a psychological perspective, there are many theories that explain our fascination with horror, ranging from the thrill of escapism to the deeper, more primal need to confront our fears.

At its core, horror taps into something ancient within us. Fear has been a survival mechanism since the dawn of humanity, keeping us alert to predators, dangers, and unknown threats. Our ancestors huddled around fires, telling terrifying stories of monsters lurking in the dark—warnings wrapped in narrative form. These stories weren't just entertainment; they were tools for survival, passing down knowledge of dangers both real and imagined. In many ways, modern horror fiction is simply an extension of this tradition. We no longer fear the beasts that prowl the night, but we do fear the collapse of society, the loss of autonomy, or the horrors hidden within the human mind. Horror allows us to explore these anxieties safely, within the confines of a story.

There is also a paradox in our love for horror—while fear is a distressing emotion, it is also exhilarating when experienced in a controlled environment. Much like the thrill of a rollercoaster, horror fiction allows us to experience adrenaline-pumping terror while knowing we are ultimately safe. This controlled fear provides an emotional rush that keeps readers hooked. But beyond the thrill, horror has a deeper function: it forces us to confront the unknown, to

1

test our emotional limits, and to imagine how we might react when faced with terrifying situations.

In this chapter, we'll explore these psychological theories, examining how horror empowers readers, making them feel both terrified and triumphant. Whether we read horror to escape, to prepare for real-life fears, or simply to experience the thrill of the unknown, the genre continues to hold an undeniable grip on our imaginations.

Psychological Theories of Fear

To understand why horror appeals to us, we first need to explore the psychology behind fear itself. Fear is not just an emotional reaction—it is a deeply ingrained survival mechanism that has helped humans navigate a dangerous world for millennia. Our ancestors relied on fear to keep them safe from predators, natural disasters, and other life-threatening dangers. While the threats have changed, our biological response to fear remains the same. Horror fiction exploits this primal response, triggering the same adrenaline rush we might experience if we were facing a real threat, yet within the safe confines of a book or film.

Sigmund Freud's concept of the uncanny is one of the most influential psychological explanations for why horror unsettles us. The uncanny refers to something that is familiar yet disturbingly strange, creating a sense of discomfort and unease. Horror frequently plays with this idea—dolls that look almost human, but not quite; shadows in the corner of our vision that may or may not be something lurking in the dark; houses that feel haunted despite no tangible evidence. When something exists in the gray area between normal and abnormal, our minds struggle to categorize it, leading to unease and fear. Freud argued that the uncanny reveals repressed fears and anxieties, making horror fiction a perfect playground for exploring the darkest corners of the subconscious mind.

Carl Jung's work on archetypes also plays a crucial role in explaining horror's power. Jung believed that the human psyche contains universal symbols—characters, themes, and motifs that appear across cultures and time periods. Among these are the archetypes of the shadow, which represents the darker side of human nature, and the monster, which embodies our fears of the unknown and the uncontrollable. These archetypes have been present in storytelling since ancient times, from the mythological beasts of Greek and Norse legend to the modern horrors of Stephen King and H.P. Lovecraft. The monster in horror fiction may be supernatural, but often it represents something much more real: societal fears, personal anxieties, or even aspects of ourselves that we'd rather not acknowledge.

Beyond Freud and Jung, modern psychology has introduced new theories to explain our love of fear. The excitation transfer theory (Dolf Zillman), for example, suggests that the heightened emotions we feel during a horror story—fear, anxiety, tension—can transform into positive emotions once the experience is over. Essentially, the fear response primes our bodies for excitement, which is why many people feel exhilarated rather than disturbed after watching a horror film or reading a particularly intense novel. Similarly, the terror management theory proposes that horror helps us cope with the fear of death by giving us a way to confront it in a symbolic form. By engaging with stories about ghosts, serial killers, or supernatural entities, we indirectly process our own mortality in a way that feels thrilling rather than overwhelming.

These psychological theories help explain why horror resonates so strongly with readers. Horror fiction takes the intangible—our deepest fears, anxieties, and existential dreads—and gives them shape, allowing us to engage with them on both a conscious and subconscious level. Whether through the uncanny, the power of archetypes, or the physiological thrill of fear, horror taps into something ancient and essential within us, making it one of the most enduring and emotionally compelling genres in literature.

Escapism vs. Confrontation

Horror offers a paradoxical experience—one that is both an escape from reality and a confrontation with our deepest fears. For many readers, horror provides a much-needed distraction from daily life. The stresses of work, relationships, and responsibilities fade into the background when we step into a world filled with supernatural threats, eerie atmospheres, and life-or-death situations. Whether it's the chilling halls of a haunted house, the desolate remains of a post-apocalyptic wasteland, or the lurking terror of an unseen predator, horror fiction transports us to a realm where reality is suspended, and anything is possible.

This sense of escapism is one of the most enjoyable aspects of horror fiction. Just as some people turn to fantasy to lose themselves in epic quests and magical realms, horror allows readers to immerse themselves in an adrenaline-fueled adventure. Even if the world inside the book is terrifying, it's still an adventure—one that carries us away from the mundane and into something far more exhilarating. There is an undeniable thrill in experiencing fear from a safe distance, much like watching a storm rage from behind a sturdy window. It allows us to experience danger without risk, heightening our emotions and pulling us into the story with an intensity that few other genres can match.

However, horror is more than just an escape. At its core, it is also a genre of confrontation—a space where we are forced to face the things we fear most. Unlike other forms of entertainment that seek to comfort or reassure, horror dares us to look directly at what unsettles us. The monsters, killers, and supernatural entities may be fictional, but the emotions they evoke are deeply real. And often, the greatest horrors in these stories are not the external threats, but the internal fears they represent.

Horror fiction provides a psychological arena where we can process our anxieties—fear of death, fear of loss, fear of the unknown—without real-world consequences. It creates a controlled environment in which we can grapple with these fears, test our reactions, and ultimately come to terms with them. When a character in a horror novel faces the dark, fights back against the monster, or endures the terror that would break a lesser person, we experience that moment alongside them. We share in their struggle, their terror, and, ultimately, their survival.

This process of vicarious survival is one of the most empowering aspects of horror. Each monster we encounter, each nightmare we endure within the pages of a book, is a symbolic battle with fear itself. And every time we turn the final page, having faced those horrors head-on, we emerge just a little stronger. In this way, horror is not just about running from fear—it is about learning to face it. The thrill of the unknown, the pulse-pounding tension, the cathartic resolution—all of these combine to make horror one of the most psychologically engaging and rewarding genres in literature.

The Heroic Journey in Horror Fiction

At its core, horror fiction often mirrors the classic heroic journey, a narrative structure where characters face overwhelming obstacles, endure harrowing trials, and emerge transformed. Unlike traditional hero's journeys, where the protagonist might acquire wisdom, power, or a sense of destiny, horror's heroes are often fighting just to survive. Yet, in that battle for survival, they experience profound psychological and emotional transformations that resonate deeply with readers.

Horror fiction is unique in that it frequently pushes characters to their absolute limits—not just physically, but mentally and emotionally. They are forced to confront their deepest fears, question their beliefs, and, in many cases, face the darkest parts of themselves. Whether they are battling supernatural creatures, deranged killers, or the horrors of their own pasts, these characters undergo trials that test their endurance, resolve, and very sense of self. This struggle is what makes horror so compelling: it presents us with characters who must fight against the unknown, and in doing so, reflect our own real-world struggles in a heightened, symbolic form.

For readers, this journey is deeply satisfying because it allows them to experience survival vicariously. Whether the protagonist overcomes the horror or succumbs to it, the reader has gone through the journey alongside them. Even in bleak horror stories where no one survives, the act of reading to the end is itself an act of endurance. The reader has faced the fear, endured the tension, and come out on the other side—perhaps a little shaken, but ultimately stronger for having taken the journey.

This is why horror is more than just a genre of fear—it is also a genre of resilience. Unlike genres where conflict exists but is not central to the emotional experience, horror is built around survival, perseverance, and the will to endure. Every horror protagonist who makes it through to the end, whether triumphant or forever changed, embodies the resilience that readers subconsciously draw from.

Horror also offers a sense of perspective on real-world struggles. In our daily lives, we face emotional, financial, and personal hardships that can feel overwhelming. But when we read about characters battling monstrous forces—whether supernatural or human—it can make our problems seem more manageable. The horror protagonist might be fleeing from a demon, trapped in a haunted asylum, or hunted by an unstoppable killer, but they keep going. They don't give up. And through them, we are reminded that we, too, can endure. For us as fans, it's similar to watching a motivational video/speech.

This is one of the reasons many readers turn to horror during difficult times. It is not because they enjoy being scared, but because horror provides a narrative of survival, a framework for understanding struggle, endurance, and, sometimes, even triumph. Whether the ending is hopeful or bleak, the journey itself is what matters. Horror fiction reminds us that fear is a challenge to be met, not something that should paralyze us.

At its best, horror does not just scare us—it empowers us. It allows us the opportunity to face the unknown, to battle our deepest fears in a safe and controlled way, and to emerge with a renewed sense of strength and resilience. And in that way, horror fiction is not just about fear—it is about overcoming it.

Our love for horror fiction stems from its ability to both terrify and empower. By tapping into deep psychological concepts like the uncanny and archetypes, horror allows us to explore primal fears in a way that feels both thrilling and cathartic. It offers us an escape from the real world, but it also gives us the tools to confront and process the fears that haunt us in everyday life. Through the lens of horror, we become not just observers but participants, joining the characters on their journey through terror and emerging stronger for it.

As we continue our exploration of the psychology of horror, we'll delve deeper into the mechanisms that make horror work—how it manipulates fear, tension, and surprise to create unforgettable experiences for readers and how writers can harness these tools to craft compelling stories.

Chapter 2

The Science of Fear

When readers encounter something frightening, the amygdala—the brain's region responsible for processing emotions, particularly fear—is activated. Upon sensing a threat, whether real or fictional, the amygdala triggers the fight-or-flight response, releasing a cascade of chemicals like adrenaline and cortisol. These hormones increase heart rate, sharpen senses, and prepare the body for action. In the context of reading horror, even though the threat isn't real, the body reacts as though it is.

Horror fiction capitalizes on this biological response by crafting narratives that exploit readers' instinctive fear reactions. The buildup of suspense, sudden twists, and unnerving settings, all work to stimulate the brain's fear center, keeping readers on edge.

But it's not just adrenaline that keeps readers hooked. After the initial scare, the brain releases dopamine, the "reward chemical." This pleasure-inducing neurotransmitter creates a sense of relief and even satisfaction after a scare. It's this balance of fear and relief that makes horror both terrifying and enjoyable. If done right, of course.

Empirical Studies on Fear Responses

Several studies have explored how individuals respond to fear-inducing stimuli, providing insights into the physiological and psychological effects of horror fiction:

- **Physiological Responses to Horror**: Research has shown that exposure to horror can trigger the fight-or-flight response, leading to increased heart rate, elevated blood pressure, and rapid breathing as adrenaline floods the system. These reactions prepare the body to confront or flee from perceived danger, even when the threat is fictional.

- **Skin Conductance and Fear**: In a study examining individuals with aphantasia (a condition where one cannot visualize mental images), researchers measured participants' fear responses by monitoring changes in skin conductivity levels—a common method to assess emotional arousal. The study found that even without visual imagery, participants exhibited physiological fear responses when exposed to scary stories, indicating that the narrative alone was sufficient to elicit a fear reaction.

- **Heart Rate Variability and Enjoyment**: An investigation into the relationship between fear and enjoyment in a haunted house setting revealed that while intense fear correlated with significant heart rate fluctuations, moderate fear levels were associated with increased enjoyment. This suggests that a balanced fear response can enhance the pleasurable aspects of horror experiences. Reminds me of folks who enjoy eating hot peppers but still stay away from the peppers that are just too hot.

- **Startle Reflex Modulation**: The fear-potentiated startle (FPS) response is a well-documented phenomenon where an individual's startle reflex is amplified in the presence of fear-inducing stimuli. Studies utilizing electromyographic recordings have demonstrated that exposure to emotionally charged content, such as horror narratives, can heighten the FPS response, providing a measurable indicator of fear. I can't even begin to tell you how many times my wife startled me while writing or reading a horror story.

These studies underscore the complex interplay between cognitive processing and physiological reactions when individuals engage with horror fiction. The body's automatic responses to perceived threats, combined with the brain's reward system, create a compelling experience that keeps readers returning to the genre.

Understanding these mechanisms not only sheds light on the allure of horror but also offers potential applications in therapeutic settings. Controlled exposure to fear-inducing stimuli, similar to the experiences found in horror fiction, may aid in desensitizing individuals to real-world fears and anxieties, providing a safe environment to confront and manage these emotions.

In essence, horror fiction serves as a unique conduit through which readers can explore the depths of fear, experience the thrill of suspense, and ultimately emerge with a sense of accomplishment and resilience.

According to research by Dr. Glenn D. Walters, horror fans are drawn to the genre because it offers what he terms "controlled fear"—a safe and structured environment where they can confront their deepest anxieties without facing real-world consequences. Walters' research highlights that horror fiction allows readers to engage with primal emotions, such as fear, dread, and suspense, within a context that they can easily control. This "safe fear" taps into our natural survival instincts, triggering the same physiological responses—like adrenaline spikes and heightened alertness—that would occur during real danger, but without any actual risk.

Additionally, Walters identifies three key elements that make horror appealing: tension, relevance, and unrealism. Tension is built through suspense, mystery, and shock, keeping readers on edge. Relevance ties into personal fears or societal anxieties, making the horror feel impactful. Unrealism, on the other hand, provides the necessary distance—ensuring that, no matter how intense the story gets, readers can remind themselves that it's all fiction.

This combination of tension, relevance, and unrealism is what makes horror such an effective tool for catharsis. It offers a way to explore the darker parts of the human psyche, confront fears, and ultimately find a sense of relief and satisfaction in surviving the narrative's horrors—all from the safety of a favorite reading chair.

Emotional and Cognitive Reactions

Beyond the immediate physiological responses like increased heart rate and adrenaline surges, horror fiction taps into deep emotional and cognitive processes that intensify the experience. Writers use psychological techniques to create a layered sense of fear, manipulating the reader's emotions and thoughts to build tension, suspense, and unease.

One of the most powerful ways horror fiction triggers emotional responses is by confronting readers with the unknown. Human beings are naturally wired to seek patterns and make sense of the world around them—this is how we navigate daily life safely and predictably. When something in a story defies these patterns, like a malevolent force without a clear motive or a monster that breaks natural laws, it disrupts our cognitive equilibrium. This cognitive dissonance—where the mind struggles to reconcile what it knows with what it is presented—leads to discomfort and fear. This is why the fear of the unknown is so potent in horror. Stories that leave questions unanswered, such as "What is that creature?" or "Why is this happening?" often evoke deeper emotional reactions than those that fully explain the threat.

Horror fiction also plays on cognitive biases, such as the negativity bias—the human tendency to focus more on negative experiences than positive ones. Writers amplify this bias by highlighting the most disturbing, dangerous, or unsettling aspects of a situation, ensuring that fear dominates the reader's mind.

For instance, a creaking door in an empty house immediately triggers thoughts of danger, even if logically there may be no threat. This taps into our survival instincts, where assuming the worst in ambiguous situations historically increased our chances of survival.

Another cognitive element that horror exploits is the theory of "mirror neurons." These are neurons in our brains that fire both when we perform an action and when we observe someone else performing it. In horror fiction, this allows readers to empathize deeply with characters in peril. When a character runs from a killer or hides from a ghost, readers experience a version of that fear themselves, as though they were there, thanks to these mirror neurons. This deepens the emotional investment in the story, making the scares more intense and personal.

Emotionally, horror fiction often plays with themes of helplessness and vulnerability—situations where characters are powerless against forces greater than themselves. This taps into a universal human fear: the loss of control. Stories like *The Shining* or *Rosemary's Baby* highlight how characters slowly lose control over their environments and even their own minds, amplifying feelings of dread and anxiety in the reader.

However, horror also manipulates hope and relief. After building intense dread, well-crafted horror stories offer moments of respite—small victories, glimmers of safety, or moments of hope. This emotional rollercoaster amplifies the cathartic effect when the story reaches its climax, whether the characters survive or succumb to the horror. The emotional journey through terror to relief is what makes horror so psychologically engaging.

In sum, horror fiction doesn't just scare us with monsters and blood—it engages our cognitive wiring and emotional depth, making us think, feel, and confront fears that might otherwise remain buried. By playing on our instinctual fears and psychological quirks, horror offers not only entertainment but also a complex emotional and intellectual experience.

Cognitive Dissonance
The Tension Between Expectation and Reality

One of the most powerful psychological tools horror fiction employs is cognitive dissonance—the mental discomfort or stress experienced when holding two conflicting ideas, beliefs, or values simultaneously. This psychological tension is a potent driver of fear and unease in horror storytelling, as it forces readers to reconcile contradictions that defy logic or challenge deeply held assumptions.

In horror fiction, cognitive dissonance often arises when something familiar is presented with an unsettling twist. For instance, a trusted character—perhaps a loving parent or a friendly neighbor—may be revealed as the villain, forcing the reader to grapple with the contradiction between the character's perceived goodness and their malevolent actions. This shattering of expectations creates a deep sense of unease because it disrupts the reader's internal narrative about trust and safety.

Another common example is the use of safe spaces turned hostile. Consider the haunted house trope—a place that should represent security and comfort becomes a source of terror. This inversion of expectation triggers cognitive dissonance, as the mind struggles to reconcile the duality of the space: it is both a home and a danger zone. This contradiction amplifies fear because it destabilizes the reader's sense of safety, leaving them unsure of what can be trusted.

Horror also uses cognitive dissonance through moral ambiguity. In stories where protagonists are forced to make ethically questionable decisions for survival, readers experience discomfort as they empathize with the character but are repulsed by their actions. For example, in *The Walking Dead*, characters must choose between preserving their humanity and doing horrific things to survive. This internal conflict mirrors the reader's own moral struggles, leading to a deeper psychological engagement with the story.

Perhaps most unsettling is when horror fiction presents scenarios that defy the laws of nature or logic. Supernatural entities that break the rules of reality—like ghosts that pass through walls or creatures that exist outside time and space—create a cognitive dissonance that taps into the primal fear of the unknown. Our brains are wired to understand the world through patterns and logic, so when horror disrupts those patterns, it triggers a deep-rooted discomfort.

This psychological tension heightens the sense of fear by placing the reader in a state of mental conflict, forcing them to question their understanding of the world. It makes horror not just a visceral experience but also an intellectual one, engaging the mind in unsettling ways that linger long after the story ends.

By exploiting cognitive dissonance, horror fiction becomes more than a simple scare—it challenges perceptions, forces readers to confront contradictions, and creates a profound sense of unease that keeps them turning the page, even as they shiver with fear.

Cognitive Biases in Horror
How Our Minds Are Manipulated for Fear

Horror fiction thrives on its ability to tap into the deepest recesses of our psychology, and one of its most effective tools is the manipulation of cognitive biases—the unconscious errors in thinking that influence how we perceive the world. By exploiting these mental shortcuts, horror authors can lead readers down paths of false assumptions, only to pull the rug out from under them, amplifying fear and unease.

Confirmation Bias and False Security: One of the most commonly exploited biases in horror is confirmation bias—our tendency to seek and interpret information in a way that confirms our existing beliefs. Horror authors skillfully use this to set traps for readers. A character might seem trustworthy, the house might appear safe, or the town might feel idyllic, leading readers to relax into a false sense of security. As the narrative progresses, unsettling truths emerge: the friendly neighbor is a killer, the house is haunted, or the perfect town hides dark secrets. This gradual unraveling forces readers to confront how easily their perceptions can be manipulated, intensifying the horror when their assumptions are shattered.

Anchoring Bias and Unreliable Narratives: Horror also capitalizes on anchoring bias—the tendency to heavily rely on the first piece of information we receive. In horror stories, early details anchor readers' expectations, but as the narrative twists, these anchors become unstable. A seemingly innocent event might later reveal a sinister undercurrent, causing readers to reframe earlier scenes in a more disturbing light. This dissonance heightens the psychological tension, as readers are forced to question what is real and what is illusion.

Jump Scares and Cognitive Traps: While often associated with visual media, jump scares in literature work through abrupt narrative shifts. A calm, detailed description of a setting suddenly erupts into chaos—a hidden monster attacks, or a character stumbles upon something grotesque. These sudden shifts prey on the brain's tendency to predict outcomes based on context, leading to a jarring dissonance when those predictions are violently upended. The unexpected leap from calm to chaos jolts the reader, triggering a fight-or-flight response and flooding the brain with adrenaline.

Cliffhangers and Heightened Alertness: Horror authors also use cliffhangers to maintain a reader's heightened state of alertness. Ending chapters with unresolved danger, mysterious discoveries, or ambiguous threats forces the reader to continue, unable to relax. This constant state of anticipation mirrors the survival instincts that keep us alert in dangerous situations, ensuring that the reader remains psychologically engaged and on edge.

The Power of the Unseen: Cognitive biases also drive our fear of the unknown. Horror often withholds information, allowing readers' imaginations to fill in the blanks. The brain, wired to seek patterns and explanations, will often conjure images far scarier than what the author might explicitly describe. This taps into the availability heuristic—a cognitive bias where people overestimate the likelihood of events based on how easily examples come to mind. By leaving details vague or hinted at, horror forces readers to envision their worst fears, making the experience deeply personal and unsettling.

By understanding and manipulating these cognitive biases, horror authors can craft stories that not only terrify but also challenge the way readers perceive reality. The genre's ability to play with our mental shortcuts, leading us into false assumptions and then breaking them apart, is what makes horror so psychologically compelling. It's not just about the monsters under the bed—it's about the monsters in our minds, and how easily they can be awakened.

Why We Keep Coming Back to Horror

Horror fiction is more than just a thrill ride—it's a psychological playground that taps into the core of human emotion and cognition. While fear is an intense and often unpleasant feeling in real life, within the safety of a book, it becomes something we can control, explore, and even enjoy.

The Thrill of Controlled Fear: At the heart of horror's appeal is the concept of "controlled fear." When we read a horror story, our brains react as though the threats are real—our hearts race, adrenaline surges, and our senses heighten. Yet, deep down, we know we're safe. This creates a unique psychological tension: the fear feels real, but the danger isn't. This controlled environment allows us to explore intense emotions without the real-world consequences, making horror a safe space to confront our anxieties.

The Relief After the Scare: One of the most fascinating aspects of the horror experience is the emotional journey it provides. After a particularly tense or terrifying scene, there's often a moment of relief—a brief respite before the next wave of fear. This release of tension triggers the brain to release dopamine, the "feel-good" chemical, leading to a sense of satisfaction and even euphoria. It's the same reason people love thrill rides or extreme sports: the rush of adrenaline followed by relief creates a powerful, addictive cycle.

The Need to Understand Fear: Another reason we return to horror is our innate curiosity about fear itself. Fear is one of the most primal human emotions, deeply tied to our survival instincts. By engaging with horror, we're not just seeking thrills—we're trying to understand what scares us and why. Horror fiction provides a space to safely explore the darkest corners of our minds, helping us confront personal and societal fears in a controlled setting.

A Sense of Mastery and Empowerment: Every time we finish a horror story, there's a subtle sense of accomplishment. We faced the monsters, the ghosts, the psychological terrors—and we survived. This feeling of mastery, even if it's purely psychological, can be incredibly empowering. It reminds us that fear, while intense, is something we can manage and overcome. This sense of control over an uncontrollable emotion is deeply satisfying and often draws readers back for more.

The Social and Cultural Connection: Horror also serves as a shared experience. Fans of the genre often connect over their favorite scary stories, discussing plot twists, shocking endings, and the deeper meanings behind the terror. This sense of community adds another layer of enjoyment, as readers bond over the stories they'd survived together. Horror taps into universal fears, creating a collective understanding that transcends cultural and personal differences.

Horror fiction is a masterclass in emotional and psychological manipulation. It activates our primal survival instincts, engages our cognitive biases, and ultimately provides a sense of control over our deepest fears. The balance between fear and relief, danger and safety, keeps readers hooked, offering a cathartic experience that resonates long after the final page is turned.

As horror writers, understanding these psychological mechanisms allows us to craft stories that don't just scare readers—they stay with them, tapping into something deeper and more profound. Horror isn't just about making people afraid; it's about helping them confront fear, understand it, and, ultimately, master it. That's why we keep coming back—because horror, in its own terrifying way, makes us feel more alive.

Chapter 3

The Therapeutic Role of Horror Fiction

Horror fiction, despite its unsettling nature, offers therapeutic benefits for readers. It serves as more than just entertainment; it becomes a tool for emotional exploration and healing. By confronting fear and danger at a safe distance, readers can address deep-seated anxieties and emerge more emotionally resilient.

Coping with Fear

Life is filled with uncertainties, anxieties, and fears—whether it's the fear of death, illness, loss, or danger. We are afraid of what we don't understand. Our natural response should be to seek knowledge, to try to make sense of the unknown so that it doesn't control us. For creative minds, especially writers and avid readers, horror fiction serves as a gateway to that understanding. It gives us a way to explore our fears in a controlled, immersive environment, where we can dissect and confront them from a safe distance.

Unlike real-life anxieties, where control often seems impossible, horror fiction provides a structured space to engage with our deepest fears. When we read about a character encountering a monster, surviving a supernatural event, or escaping a masked killer, we're also engaging with our own internal fears. Horror stories create a psychological buffer between us and real-world horrors, allowing us to prepare for life's inevitable tragedies, like the loss of a loved one. By watching fictional characters endure and react to terror, we are rehearsing our own emotional responses.

This is one of the reasons we're drawn to horror stories about survival and resilience. We don't just want to witness fear—we want to see how it's overcome. Every time a protagonist battles a nightmare scenario, fights back, and survives, it reassures us that survival is possible. And when characters don't make it, those stories act as cautionary tales, warning us about dangers we might encounter in our own lives. Horror fiction, in this way, becomes an emotional simulator, helping us mentally and emotionally prepare for the worst without experiencing real-life consequences.

Beyond survival instincts, horror also offers catharsis. We all carry anxieties and stress, and horror gives us a way to release them. It's why people scream on rollercoasters or jump at a haunted house attraction but walk away laughing. The adrenaline rush, followed by relief, is a powerful emotional reset. Similarly, in horror fiction, we go through fear and dread in a structured way, leading to a sense of release when the story ends. Even if a book leaves us unsettled, there's still satisfaction in having faced the darkness and emerged, in a sense, victorious.

Horror fiction isn't just about scares—it's about confronting and making peace with our own fears. It provides a space where we can safely explore mortality, danger, and the unknown. By immersing ourselves in these stories, we aren't just seeking entertainment—we're seeking a deeper understanding of fear itself. And in understanding fear, we rob it of some of its power.

The Role of Horror in Coping with Grief

Grief is one of the most profound and universal human experiences, often leaving individuals grappling with questions of mortality, loss, and meaning. Horror fiction, with its raw exploration of fear, death, and the unknown, offers a unique avenue for processing these emotions. By delving into the dark corners of human existence, horror provides a cathartic space to confront grief and loss, offering solace and understanding in unexpected ways.

Confronting Mortality Through Horror

At its core, horror often revolves around the ultimate fear: death. Whether through tales of vengeful spirits, grotesque monsters, or apocalyptic scenarios, the genre forces readers to face the fragility of life. This confrontation with mortality can be paradoxically comforting. By engaging with stories that dramatize and externalize the fear of death, readers can explore their anxieties in a controlled, imaginative space.

Stories like Stephen King's *Pet Sematary* embody this struggle, weaving a narrative that explores the lengths to which people will go to avoid the pain of losing loved ones. The horror arises not just from the supernatural elements but from the devastating emotional truth at its heart: the desperate, human yearning to defy death.

Grief as a Catalyst for Horror Narratives

Horror fiction frequently uses grief as a starting point for its stories. Protagonists who have experienced profound loss often become the emotional anchor of a narrative, allowing readers to empathize with their pain. This grief-driven storytelling mirrors the real-world process of mourning, where loss often gives rise to introspection, change, and even transformation.

Take Mike Flanagan's *The Haunting of Hill House* adaptation as an example. The story uses the Crain family's shared trauma and individual grief as the foundation for its supernatural horror. The ghosts haunting Hill House become metaphors for the unresolved pain and guilt each family member carries, illustrating how grief can linger and fester if left unaddressed.

Processing Grief Through Horror's Framework

Horror fiction offers a way to explore grief without directly confronting it. The genre allows readers to project their emotions onto fantastical scenarios, giving them the freedom to process complex feelings at a safe distance. The metaphorical nature of horror—monsters as fears, hauntings as unresolved trauma—provides a powerful framework for understanding loss.

For example, *The Babadook* uses the titular monster as a manifestation of a mother's grief over losing her husband. The film's horror is rooted in the psychological torment of mourning and the struggle to move forward. By externalizing grief in the form of a tangible threat, the story makes the abstract pain of loss feel more manageable, even conquerable.

Building Resilience Through Fear

Engaging with horror fiction can also foster resilience. By confronting fear and grief in a controlled environment, readers build emotional endurance. This concept ties into the therapeutic role of horror: the more individuals face their anxieties in fictional scenarios, the better equipped they are to handle real-world challenges.

Horror fiction's ability to offer a sense of resolution is particularly meaningful for those coping with grief. While not all horror stories end happily, many provide closure, redemption, or understanding. These endings can mirror the journey of grief, reinforcing the idea that, while pain is inevitable, healing is possible.

Horror's Universality in Addressing Loss

The fear of death and the pain of loss transcend cultures, making grief a universal theme in horror. Different cultures approach these themes through their unique traditions and beliefs. Japanese horror often emphasizes the lingering presence of the dead, as seen in *The Grudge*, while Mexican folklore, exemplified by *La Llorona*, explores themes of mourning and justice. These cultural variations highlight how horror can reflect and address the universal human experience of loss.

Horror as a Safe Haven for Grief

Horror fiction offers more than scares; it provides a space to process the unthinkable. By confronting death and loss through the lens of horror, readers and viewers can navigate the complexities of grief with a sense of distance and safety. These stories validate the pain of loss while reminding us of our shared humanity and the resilience we carry within.

Whether through ghostly hauntings, monstrous manifestations, or psychological terrors, horror's exploration of grief is a testament to its power as a genre. It allows us to face the darkest parts of life, ultimately emerging stronger, more empathetic, and better equipped to cope with the inevitabilities of the human experience.

Facing Personal Fears

Horror fiction allows us to look our fears in the eye—safely. In the pages of a book or on the screen, terrifying things happen, but we, as readers, remain in control. This gives horror a unique psychological power: it creates distance between us and our trauma, while still letting us engage with it on an emotional level. In doing so, horror becomes a powerful tool for personal reflection and healing.

The monsters, spirits, and grotesque entities that haunt horror stories are rarely just literal threats. They often symbolize deeper anxieties—things we fear in our own lives but struggle to name or confront. Fear of losing a loved one, fear of being powerless, fear of mental illness, or even the dread of isolation or failure. These real-world concerns take shape as supernatural antagonists or creeping psychological dread. For readers dealing with those same emotions, horror fiction can feel like both a mirror and a guide.

Stephen King's *Carrie* offers a striking example. The story of a bullied, misunderstood teen with telekinetic powers resonates deeply with anyone who has felt marginalized or powerless. Readers who see parts of themselves in Carrie—especially in her pain, alienation, or loss of control—may find catharsis in her eventual transformation. Even if the ending is tragic, the emotional journey speaks to the universal longing for strength and recognition.

Horror also gives readers permission to explore fears they may otherwise avoid. Whether it's the terror of death, the burden of guilt, or the trauma of abuse, horror fiction offers metaphors that make these difficult emotions easier to approach. The genre invites us to grapple with big, uncomfortable questions in a manageable way: What would I do in that situation? What am I really afraid of? And could I survive it?

Importantly, horror doesn't just dwell on fear—it often celebrates survival. Seeing characters face their worst nightmares and emerge transformed (even if scarred) offers readers a sense of validation. It tells them that their fears are real, but also that fear can be endured, processed, and even overcome. In this way, horror fiction becomes a form of emotional rehearsal, allowing readers to confront their own demons—and perhaps leave the story a little stronger than they were before.

Catharsis and Resilience

One of the most powerful psychological functions of horror fiction is its ability to offer catharsis—a release of intense emotion that provides a sense of relief and renewal. Readers often enter a horror story carrying their own stress, fears, or frustrations, and by the end of the journey, they've processed those emotions alongside the characters. The fright, tension, and ultimate resolution serve as a safe outlet for real-life anxiety, anger, grief, or helplessness. That pulse-pounding sequence where the protagonist narrowly escapes a monster or uncovers the truth behind a haunting? It's not just entertainment—it's a mechanism for emotional release.

This is not just theoretical. Psychologists have observed that controlled exposure to fear (similar to techniques used in exposure therapy) can help individuals become less reactive to stress and more confident in their ability to handle adversity. Horror stories, by simulating danger, offer a version of this therapy—especially when the fear is tied to real emotional struggles like loneliness, loss, guilt, or insecurity.

Authors like Shirley Jackson (*The Haunting of Hill House*) and H.P. Lovecraft (*The Shadow Over Innsmouth*) delve into complex emotional and existential fears. Their characters often grapple with madness, isolation, or the weight of unknowable truths. As readers follow these journeys, they not only witness terror unfold—they engage with the same questions and anxieties that plague them in real life.

In the end, horror fiction isn't just about the scare—it's about what happens after the scare. That exhale of relief, that heartbeat slowing down, that strange sense of clarity or empowerment. Horror gives readers permission to explore their darkest thoughts, and more importantly, it shows them that those thoughts can be faced. By surviving the horror on the page, they're better equipped to survive what haunts them off the page, too.

Chapter 4

Horror as a Reflection of Society

Horror fiction, in many ways, serves as a mirror for society's deepest fears and anxieties. Throughout history, societal shifts, cultural traumas, and existential crises have all been reflected in horror stories. By analyzing the evolution of horror and its themes, we can see how the genre responds to and reflects the concerns of its time.

At its core, horror is a genre that thrives on fear—specifically, the fears that permeate the collective consciousness at any given moment in history. These fears are often rooted in real societal issues: war, disease, technological advancements, political unrest, and cultural shifts. As society changes, so too do its anxieties, and horror fiction adapts to capture these evolving tensions.

For instance, during the Cold War era, horror was rife with themes of paranoia and the fear of the "other." Films like *Invasion of the Body Snatchers* (1956) captured the widespread fear of infiltration—whether by communists or aliens—highlighting the anxiety surrounding identity, trust, and the loss of autonomy. Similarly, the 1980s saw a wave of body horror films, such as David Cronenberg's *The Fly* (1986), reflecting society's growing fear of disease and the AIDS epidemic, as well as anxieties surrounding rapid technological advancements and the human body's fragility.

Friday the 13th can be seen as a reflection of 1980s moral and cultural anxieties, particularly around sex and punishment. In the film, teens who engage in sexual activity are often the first to die, reinforcing the trope that "sex equals death." This mirrored the era's growing fears surrounding the AIDS crisis and may also reflect conservative messaging around abstinence, which gained traction during the Reagan era. Whether intentional or not, the film taps into a societal fear of consequence tied to pleasure, presenting Jason as a symbolic enforcer of repressive moral codes.

In more recent times, horror has turned its gaze toward social issues, exploring systemic racism, inequality, and cultural tensions. Jordan Peele's *Get Out* (2017) is a prime example, using horror as a tool to explore and critique deep-seated racial anxieties and the concept of cultural appropriation. This shift reflects a growing awareness in society of social justice issues and the desire to confront uncomfortable truths through storytelling.

As authors, it is crucial to stay attuned to these societal shifts and understand how collective fears evolve. Horror writers are often at the forefront of cultural commentary, using their work to shine a light on the darkest corners of society. By keeping a finger on the pulse of societal change, authors can craft stories that not only terrify but also resonate on a deeper, more meaningful level.

But horror isn't just reactive—it can also be predictive. Great horror fiction doesn't just reflect current fears; it anticipates them. Authors who delve into speculative horror, for example, often explore the potential consequences of current societal trends, warning readers about what might happen if these trends spiral out of control. George Orwell's *1984* and Ray Bradbury's *Fahrenheit 451* are classic examples of speculative fiction that, while not strictly horror, use dystopian elements to forecast terrifying societal shifts. In the horror genre, stories that predict the dangers of unchecked technology, like *Black Mirror*, play on present anxieties while also imagining future horrors.

This predictive element is vital for horror authors. We must not only respond to current societal fears but also consider where those fears might lead. This requires a keen understanding of cultural movements, emerging technologies, political climates, and even psychological shifts within society. By anticipating the next big cultural anxiety, authors can create stories that feel eerily prescient and deeply unsettling.

Nostalgia also plays a significant role in how horror reflects society. As much as horror adapts to new fears, it often cycles back to older tropes, reimagining them for modern audiences. Classic horror elements—haunted houses, vampires, werewolves—continue to find relevance, often used as allegories for contemporary issues. The resurgence of retro horror, like Netflix's *Stranger Things*, capitalizes on this nostalgia, blending 1980s aesthetics with modern storytelling to create something both familiar and fresh. This nostalgia taps into readers' emotional connections to past eras, while still reflecting current fears and societal shifts.

As horror authors, we can use this nostalgia to our advantage. By reimagining classic tropes with modern twists, we can appeal to readers' sense of familiarity while still providing new and unsettling experiences. This approach allows us to bridge the gap between old and new fears, creating stories that feel timeless yet relevant.

Horror also offers readers a safe space to process societal trauma. During times of crisis, whether it's war, economic collapse, or a global pandemic, horror fiction provides a cathartic outlet. It allows readers to confront collective anxieties in a controlled environment, offering a sense of understanding and even empowerment. Stories like Stephen King's *The Stand* or Emily St. John Mandel's *Station Eleven* explore themes of pandemic and societal collapse, giving readers a way to process real-world fears through fiction.

In essence, horror serves as both a reflection and a prediction of society's darkest fears. It reacts to cultural shifts while also speculating on where those shifts might lead. As authors, we play a crucial role in this process. By staying informed, observing societal changes, and daring to imagine the consequences of current trends, we can craft stories that not only terrify but also provoke thought and spark dialogue.

Horror fiction isn't just about monsters and ghosts—it's about us. It's about what we fear, what we value, and what we are willing to confront in the dark corners of our minds and societies. As horror writers, we stand at the intersection of imagination and reality, using our craft to hold up a mirror to the world and ask, "What if?"

Societal Fears and Cultural Anxieties

Horror fiction has always served as a lens through which society examines its deepest and often unspoken fears. It magnifies the anxieties that simmer beneath the surface, giving them tangible forms—whether they be monsters, apocalyptic worlds, or the breakdown of the self. One of the most common and enduring themes in horror is the fear of the "other," but this is just one of many societal fears that horror fiction exploits to both terrify and provoke thought.

Fear of the "Other": The concept of the "other" is a powerful driver in horror fiction. It manifests as creatures, outsiders, or forces that challenge the norms of society and threaten the status quo. These "others" often represent marginalized groups, foreign ideologies, or even repressed aspects of the self. In Bram Stoker's *Dracula*, the vampire isn't merely a bloodsucking monster—he symbolizes Victorian-era anxieties about immigration, disease, and sexual deviance. Dracula, with his foreign origin and seductive nature, played on cultural fears about contamination—both physical (through blood and disease) and moral (through sexuality and corruption).

This theme of the "other" extends into modern horror as well. Films like *The Thing* (1982) use shape-shifting aliens to explore Cold War-era paranoia and the fear of infiltration—who can you trust when the enemy could be anyone? Similarly, Jordan Peele's *Get Out* (2017) uses horror to expose the insidiousness of systemic racism, where the "other" is the protagonist himself, navigating a world that sees him as an outsider in ways he initially doesn't realize.

Fear of Social Collapse: Another prevalent theme in horror is the fear of societal breakdown—the collapse of the structures that keep chaos at bay. This fear has been explored extensively in post-apocalyptic fiction, where the veneer of civilization is stripped away to reveal humanity's baser instincts.

In *The Road* by Cormac McCarthy, the post-apocalyptic setting is bleak and stripped of any hope, forcing characters into a survivalist nightmare. The horror doesn't come from monsters or supernatural forces but from humanity itself—desperation turning people into predators. Similarly, zombie films like *28 Days Later* (2002) reflect fears of pandemics and societal collapse, where a virus doesn't just kill but obliterates the very fabric of society, forcing survivors into lawless chaos.

This theme resonates because it taps into our primal fear of losing control and being thrust into a brutal, survivalist world. It asks a haunting question: without the rules and structures of civilization, who are we really? This exploration of moral decay and the fragility of societal order is a core element in many horror narratives.

Fear of Technology and Modernization: As society has become increasingly reliant on technology, horror fiction has adapted to reflect anxieties surrounding these advancements. Stories about artificial intelligence, surveillance, and the erosion of privacy have become central to modern horror. Films like *Ex Machina* (2014) delve into the ethical and existential dilemmas of creating life through technology, while *Black Mirror* consistently explores the dark side of humanity's relationship with tech—highlighting fears about losing control over the very tools we've created.

This fear of technology isn't new, but it has evolved with society. Where Mary Shelley's *Frankenstein* warned against the unchecked ambition of scientific discovery, modern stories now ask: What happens when technology knows us better than we know ourselves? Horror explores this discomfort, forcing readers to question the safety of the digital age.

Fear of Personal Identity Crisis: One of the most unsettling societal fears explored in horror fiction is the breakdown of personal identity. As the pressures of modern life mount—social expectations, mental health struggles, and cultural alienation—horror stories have begun to delve deeper into the psyche, exploring how fragile the sense of self can be.

Films like *Black Swan* (2010) and *Hereditary* (2018) highlight this theme by focusing on protagonists whose realities fracture under pressure. In *Black Swan*, Nina's descent into madness is driven by the intense pressure to achieve perfection, leading to a loss of self that blurs the line between reality and hallucination. *Hereditary*, on the other hand, explores inherited trauma and familial curses, symbolizing how personal identity can be shaped—and destroyed—by forces beyond our control.

These narratives reflect a growing societal focus on mental health and the struggle to maintain identity in an increasingly complex and demanding world. The horror comes not from external threats, but from within—suggesting that sometimes the scariest place to be is inside one's own mind.

Fear of the Environment and Global Catastrophe: As concerns about climate change and environmental destruction grow, horror fiction has begun to explore ecological fears. Eco-horror stories like Jeff VanderMeer's *Annihilation* (2014) delve into the terrifying unknowns of nature and humanity's impact on it. In *Annihilation*, nature mutates in inexplicable ways, reflecting humanity's fear of losing control over the environment and the unintended consequences of scientific exploration.

These narratives once again serve as cautionary tales, forcing readers to confront the reality of environmental degradation and its potential to disrupt life as we know it. By turning nature into the antagonist, eco-horror taps into the anxiety that the planet itself may eventually turn against us—a fear that feels increasingly plausible in today's world.

Blending Fears for Maximum Impact: One of horror fiction's greatest strengths is its ability to blend multiple societal fears into a single narrative, creating a layered, complex story that resonates on multiple levels. *The Walking Dead* franchise, for example, is not just about zombies—it's about the collapse of society, the fragility of morality, and the fear of the "other" (both in the form of the undead and surviving humans). It examines how quickly humanity can lose its sense of civility when the structures we rely on fall apart.

Similarly, *Us* (2019) by Jordan Peele explores themes of duality and privilege, where the protagonists confront their doppelgängers—literal representations of their repressed selves and societal inequalities. It's a story that blends fears of the "other" with a deeper reflection on classism and the darkness that exists within everyone.

The Author's Role in Reflecting and Predicting Fear: As horror authors, we are not just storytellers—we are chroniclers of fear. Our job is to not only reflect the anxieties of the time but also to anticipate and predict emerging fears. This requires staying attuned to cultural shifts, technological advancements, and societal trends. By understanding what makes people uneasy today, we can craft stories that tap into those fears, amplifying them into compelling narratives.

At the same time, horror writers also shape the conversation around fear. By exploring new societal anxieties, we push readers to confront uncomfortable truths—about society, about others, and about themselves. We play a crucial role in both reflecting and shaping cultural consciousness.

And let's not forget the power of nostalgia. Readers often find comfort in familiar horror tropes—haunted houses, vampires, zombies—not because they're inherently less scary, but because they offer a sense of connection to the past. These classic elements can be reimagined in modern ways to appeal to both new readers and those who long for the horrors they grew up with. As writers, blending nostalgia with fresh ideas allows us to craft stories that feel both timeless and relevant.

The Role of Horror in Modern Culture: More Than Just Scares: In today's complex world, horror has transcended its roots as simple entertainment to become a potent cultural force—one that helps society process chaos, violence, and the darker aspects of the human experience. Far from being just stories designed to scare, modern horror serves as a mirror, a coping mechanism, and a tool for social critique. It provides audiences with a means to understand and confront the fears that permeate our collective consciousness.

Adapting to New Anxieties

As we established, Horror fiction's ability to evolve alongside society's fears is one of the reasons it remains such a relevant and popular genre. As the world changes, so do the things that terrify us, and horror adapts to reflect those shifting anxieties. While early horror often dealt with survival in the wilderness, contemporary horror digs deeper into psychological and existential fears—fears that are harder to escape because they exist within us or the very fabric of our society.

In the past, horror fiction often revolved around tangible threats: monsters, ghosts, and the wilderness itself. These stories reflected a time when survival against natural forces or supernatural beings was at the forefront of human anxiety. Unlike today, they didn't understand what a whirlwind, earthquake, or other types of natural phenomena was. We tend to fear what we don't understand.

As technology advanced and societies became more complex, so did the fears that horror explored. The Cold War era brought with it fears of nuclear annihilation, leading to horror films like *Invasion of the Body Snatchers* and *Godzilla*, where the monstrous represented the lurking dangers of science and technology gone wrong.

As our understanding of psychology deepened in the 20th century, horror shifted toward more internalized fears. The genre began to explore mental illness, isolation, and the fragility of the human mind. Stories like *Psycho* and *The Shining* introduced readers to horror rooted in psychological breakdowns, blurring the lines between what is real and imagined. The fear of losing control, whether to external forces or internal madness, became a central theme in modern horror. It still is to this very day.

Horror continues to evolve in response to the anxieties of the times. In the age of technology and social media, we see horror that deals with surveillance, loss of privacy, and the erosion of individual identity. Dystopian stories like *The Handmaid's Tale* and *Black Mirror* tap into fears of societal collapse, oppression, and the rise of totalitarian regimes. These stories reflect growing concerns around technology, government control, and the loss of personal freedom. Similarly, AI-driven horror stories are on the rise, questioning the consequences of artificial intelligence, deepfakes, and the manipulation of reality itself.

Another modern trend in horror is the exploration of existential threats, such as climate change or pandemics. As we face an uncertain future, horror fiction provides a space for writers and readers to grapple with these overwhelming anxieties. Whether it's eco-horror, where nature turns against humanity, or pandemic horror, where invisible threats bring society to its knees, these stories provide both a reflection of our fears and a way to process them.

But even as horror constantly evolves, older trends don't fade away—they become classics. The gothic horror of *Dracula* and *Frankenstein*, once cutting-edge, now stands as foundational works that continue to influence the genre. The haunted house trope, perfected by *The Haunting of Hill House*, is still widely used, its familiar structure providing comfort while simultaneously unnerving us. Slasher films, while evolving, retain the core formula that made *Halloween* and *Friday the 13th* cult phenomena.

As mentioned earlier, nostalgia plays a huge role in horror storytelling. Readers and viewers often seek out familiar tropes, relishing the comfort of the stories they grew up with. This is why we see revivals of 80s-style horror like *Stranger Things* and remakes of classic horror films. We're already starting to see more and more 90s nostalgia being presented to us. These narratives provide both a return to the fears of childhood and a new interpretation for modern audiences. As horror writers, we can tap into this desire for the familiar while twisting it in unexpected ways, breathing new life into well-worn fears.

As authors, we are at the forefront of this evolution. We are the ones shaping the next wave of horror, interpreting the world around us through the lens of fear. Whether we choose to draw on contemporary anxieties, reinvent classic tropes, or experiment with entirely new horror landscapes, we play a vital role in reflecting and shaping the collective fears of our time.

Historical Roots of Fear in Fiction

Fear, as a universal human experience, has always been a powerful force in storytelling. From the earliest myths to the modern horror genre, the way we confront fear through fiction has evolved alongside society itself. Horror fiction, in particular, has adapted to reflect the changing fears of each era, responding to cultural anxieties and the shifting landscapes of human experience. In this chapter, we'll explore how horror has developed over time, from ancient myths to Gothic novels and modern-day psychological horror, and how it continues to evolve in response to society's evolving fears.

The origins of horror fiction can be traced back to early myths and folklore, where stories often served as cautionary tales to protect communities from danger. In ancient times, people told stories of vengeful gods, spirits, and monsters—beings that embodied the forces of nature, morality, and the unknown. These early horror tales, whether it was the terrifying Greek myth of Medusa or the Norse tale of Fenrir, were rooted in the mysteries of life, death, and survival. In many cultures, these stories were passed down through generations as a way to warn against the dangers lurking in the world, be they natural or supernatural.

One of the earliest known written horror stories is the *Epic of Gilgamesh*, dating back to around 1800 BCE in Mesopotamia.

This ancient epic includes themes of mortality, the afterlife, and encounters with frightening deities, reflecting humanity's early attempts to grapple with existential fears.

Another significant early work is "Beowulf," an Old English epic poem believed to have been composed between the 8th and 11th centuries. One of my personal favorites, actually. It tells the story of the hero Beowulf and his battles against the monster Grendel, Grendel's mother, and a dragon. While primarily a tale of heroism, Beowulf incorporates elements of horror through its monstrous antagonists and dark, foreboding settings.

As societies grew more complex, so did their stories. The rise of Gothic literature in the 18th and 19th centuries marked a significant turning point in horror fiction. Novels like Mary Shelley's *Frankenstein* and Bram Stoker's *Dracula* introduced readers to new kinds of fears—fears born from science, the unknown, and the unnatural. These Gothic tales combined the eerie, isolated settings of old folklore with a modern fascination with morality, the supernatural, and human fallibility. The crumbling castles, dark forests, and desolate landscapes of Gothic fiction became the perfect backdrop for exploring the anxieties of a changing world, where religion, science, and society were all undergoing upheaval.

The 20th century saw the rise of pulp horror and the eventual mainstreaming of horror fiction. Authors like H.P. Lovecraft and Edgar Allan Poe brought psychological horror to the forefront, introducing existential dread and cosmic horror into the mix. In their stories, the monsters were often not just physical beings but the terrifying vastness of the unknown itself. Lovecraft's tales of ancient gods and incomprehensible forces introduced readers to the fear that humanity is insignificant in the grand scheme of the universe, a theme that continues to haunt modern horror fiction.

With the arrival of Stephen King, Clive Barker, and modern horror cinema, horror expanded to include everything from supernatural thrillers to grotesque body horror and slasher films. Horror's reach into the mainstream allowed it to explore new fears, from the terror of being hunted to the dread of isolation, both physical and emotional. Modern horror also began to shift focus from external monsters to internal ones, creating a space where psychological horror could flourish.

Chapter 5

Exploring the Boundaries of Fiction and Imagination

One of the most profound aspects of horror fiction is its unique ability to stretch the limits of human imagination. Unlike other genres that often stay grounded in reality or follow established rules, horror thrives on breaking those rules, leading readers into uncharted and terrifying territories. By stepping beyond the bounds of the real world, horror invites readers to explore the darkest corners of their minds, confronting fears and scenarios they may never encounter in real life. Imagination in horror is not just a tool—it's the gateway to experiencing terror in its most raw and visceral form.

At its core, horror fiction taps into the unknown—the realm of things that defy explanation or logic. It asks readers to envision realities where the impossible becomes possible, where the dead rise, the mind fractures, and ancient evils lurk just beyond the veil of perception. Consider H.P. Lovecraft's Cthulhu Mythos, where the monsters aren't just grotesque and powerful—they're incomprehensible. These cosmic horrors challenge the limits of human understanding, evoking fear not only because they're dangerous but because they represent something unknowable. Lovecraft's work forces readers to let go of rationality, diving into a universe where humanity is insignificant and powerless in the face of ancient, godlike beings.

Another example of imagination pushing boundaries is in Clive Barker's *Hellraiser*. The Cenobites, led by the iconic Pinhead, aren't simple monsters—they are explorers of extreme sensations, blending pain and pleasure in ways that challenge moral and physical boundaries. The story asks readers to imagine a world where the lines between pleasure, pain, life, and death blur, creating a visceral and deeply disturbing experience. Barker's twisted imagination forces readers to confront taboos and consider how far one might go in the pursuit of ultimate experience.

Imagination in horror also extends to the psychological. In Stephen King's *The Shining*, the Overlook Hotel becomes a living, breathing entity, feeding off the trauma and madness of its inhabitants. The horrors Jack Torrance faces are as much internal as they are external. The hotel becomes a manifestation of his crumbling psyche, turning familiar spaces into sources of terror. This manipulation of imagination—where ordinary places become sinister—taps into the uncanny, unsettling readers by distorting their sense of reality.

Movies, too, have pushed the boundaries of horror through imagination. *The Thing* (1982) showcases a shapeshifting alien that can mimic any living organism. The fear isn't just of the creature itself but the paranoia it induces—anyone could be the monster. This challenges the audience's perception of reality, creating a tense atmosphere where trust is impossible. Similarly, *A Nightmare on Elm Street* (1984) plays with the concept of dreams, where the antagonist Freddy Krueger attacks teenagers in their sleep. The film blurs the line between reality and dreams, forcing viewers to question what is real and what isn't, making even sleep—a safe, everyday act—a terrifying vulnerability.

Stephen King famously said, "We make up horrors to help us cope with the real ones." Imagination in horror allows readers and viewers to confront real-world fears by transforming them into something exaggerated, fantastical, or grotesque. It gives shape to intangible anxieties—death, isolation, loss of control—by turning them into something visible and (at least within the story) conquerable.

Horror's imaginative power also allows for deep metaphorical storytelling. Jordan Peele's *Get Out* uses horror to explore systemic racism, embedding real societal fears within the framework of a suspenseful, terrifying narrative. The Armitage family's seemingly idyllic house becomes a nightmare of exploitation and control, with the "Sunken Place" serving as a powerful metaphor for the voicelessness and helplessness experienced by the protagonist. Peele's imaginative approach turns abstract social issues into tangible horror, forcing viewers to confront uncomfortable truths.

Even in literature aimed at younger audiences, imagination plays a critical role in horror. R.L. Stine's Goosebumps series introduces children to safe, imaginative horror, where haunted masks, ventriloquist dummies, and spooky basements become sources of terror. These stories allow young readers to explore fear in manageable doses, helping them develop coping mechanisms for anxiety and building resilience through fictional scares.

Imagination also plays a role in how horror subverts expectations. In *The Cabin in the Woods*, what starts as a typical slasher film quickly devolves into a meta-commentary on the horror genre itself. The movie imagines a world where all horror tropes are part of a larger ritual, turning familiar conventions into something new and disturbing. It asks viewers to reconsider the boundaries between fiction and reality, forcing them to confront the role they play as consumers of horror.

Ultimately, horror's ability to stretch the imagination is what makes it so powerful. It gives readers and viewers a space to confront fears—both personal and societal—in ways that are impossible in the real world. Whether it's through cosmic horrors, psychological breakdowns, or social commentary, horror challenges us to envision the unimaginable and, in doing so, helps us make sense of the chaos and darkness that exist both within and around us.

In the next section, we'll explore how horror plays with the boundary between fiction and reality—blurring the lines so effectively that, at times, the fear feels all too real.

When Fiction Becomes Too Real

Horror fiction often thrives on the delicate balance between fiction and reality, blurring the lines just enough to make the reader question what's possible. By grounding terrifying events in familiar settings or believable scenarios, horror intensifies its impact, making the fear feel immediate and deeply personal. When fiction becomes "too real," it taps into our subconscious anxieties, making the horror more unsettling and harder to shake off.

One of the most effective ways horror does this is by placing the supernatural or the horrific into everyday contexts, creating a jarring contrast between the ordinary and the terrifying. Take Shirley Jackson's *The Haunting of Hill House* as a prime example. While the story revolves around a haunted house, the true horror stems from the psychological unraveling of the protagonist, Eleanor. The house isn't just haunted by spirits—it becomes a reflection of Eleanor's inner turmoil, loneliness, and emotional fragility. Jackson masterfully blurs the lines between supernatural horror and psychological breakdown, leaving readers unsure of what's real and what exists solely in Eleanor's mind. This ambiguity makes the story more terrifying because it taps into the fear of losing control over one's own thoughts and perceptions.

Another powerful example is *The Exorcist* by William Peter Blatty. The story of young Regan MacNeil's demonic possession is deeply disturbing, not because demonic possession is common or even believed by all readers, but because it intersects with universal fears—loss of control, the vulnerability of children, and the intrusion of evil into safe spaces. The horror is magnified by its grounding in religious themes and psychological realism. The idea that a child's body could be overtaken by an unseen force strikes at the core of parental anxieties and societal fears of corruption and innocence lost. The fact that *The Exorcist* was inspired by an alleged real-life exorcism only adds another layer of unease, forcing readers to question the boundary between fiction and reality.

Horror often feels most potent when it draws from real-life fears and anxieties. Consider *The Silence of the Lambs* by Thomas Harris, where the horror doesn't stem from ghosts or monsters but from the mind of a brilliant, cannibalistic psychiatrist, Hannibal Lecter, and the actions of a serial killer, Buffalo Bill. The idea that such evil could exist within the guise of normalcy—hidden behind a charming smile or within a seemingly mundane suburban home—plays on the fear that danger could be lurking anywhere. Because serial killers are a real, documented phenomenon, the story's horror feels grounded and intensely plausible.

Films have also capitalized on this blending of reality and fiction. *The Blair Witch Project* (1999) is a classic example of horror fiction that feels "too real." Marketed as found footage from a group of missing filmmakers, the movie blurs the lines between documentary and fiction. Its low-budget, shaky-camera style gave audiences the impression that they were watching real events unfold, amplifying the fear factor. Many viewers believed the story was true upon its release, demonstrating how easily horror can manipulate perception when it mimics reality.

Another example is *Hereditary* (2018), where the horror begins as a family drama about grief and loss before spiraling into supernatural terror. The initial focus on realistic themes—grieving a loved one, family dysfunction, and mental illness—grounds the narrative in the real world, making the eventual supernatural elements feel even more jarring and disturbing. The film forces viewers to question whether the haunting events are supernatural or manifestations of inherited psychological trauma, leaving them in a state of unease long after the credits roll.

Horror writers often play on this thin line between fiction and reality by incorporating real-world fears into their narratives. Stories about pandemics (*The Stand* by Stephen King), home invasions (*The Strangers*), or societal collapse (*The Road* by Cormac McCarthy) tap into existing anxieties and amplify them through fictional storytelling. These scenarios are terrifying not because they are entirely implausible but because they feel like they could happen—or in some cases, have happened. This reflection of real-world fears through the distorted lens of fiction creates a unique psychological tension, making readers question the safety and stability of their own lives.

One technique that enhances this blending is the use of ambiguous endings or unreliable narrators, which leave readers questioning the reality of the events they've just witnessed. In *The Turn of the Screw* by Henry James, the reader is left wondering whether the governess truly saw ghosts or was descending into madness. This ambiguity forces readers to fill in the gaps, using their own imagination and fears to interpret the story, which often leads to an even more unsettling experience.

The fear of the "unseen" is another powerful tool in horror. Films like *Paranormal Activity* use minimal special effects, relying instead on subtle movements, shadows, and sounds to suggest the presence of a malevolent force. This plays into the psychological fear of the unknown—what we can't see is often more terrifying than what we can. The mind fills in the blanks, sometimes conjuring horrors far worse than anything a filmmaker or writer could depict explicitly.

Ultimately, the most effective horror stories are those that walk the tightrope between fiction and reality, creating scenarios that feel plausible enough to unsettle us but imaginative enough to captivate. When horror becomes "too real," it forces readers and viewers to confront their own fears in a deeply personal way, blurring the lines between what's safe and what's threatening.

In the next chapter, we'll explore how horror authors use psychological principles to craft stories that not only terrify but also manipulate emotions, build tension, and keep readers hooked from the first page to the last.

The Art of Blurring the Lines

At its core, horror fiction thrives on its ability to dance on the thin line between reality and imagination, making readers question what is possible and what is purely the product of a dark, creative mind. The genre's most compelling stories pull us into worlds where the impossible feels just plausible enough to send shivers down our spines. Horror authors are masters at crafting these illusions, stretching the limits of our imaginations while anchoring the terror in recognizable, sometimes painfully familiar settings.

This delicate balance between the real and the fantastical is what gives horror its unique psychological punch. When fiction mirrors the fears we already harbor—be it societal collapse, personal loss, or the darkness within ourselves—it becomes far more impactful. But horror doesn't stop there. It also challenges us to venture into uncharted territories of fear, exploring cosmic horrors, supernatural forces, and twisted psychological landscapes that stretch our minds beyond their comfort zones.

The art of blurring these boundaries invites readers to not only confront their fears but also to reflect on the fragile nature of reality itself. Is the monster under the bed a figment of our imagination, or a representation of a deeper, more personal fear? Is the haunted house truly cursed, or is it the manifestation of guilt and trauma? These questions are what make horror fiction so enduring and deeply psychological—it forces us to confront the things we'd rather keep hidden.

I've said it before and I'll say it again... Horror offers a safe but thrilling space to explore the darkest parts of human existence. It reminds us that the scariest monsters aren't always the ones lurking in the shadows—they're often the ones that exist within our own minds or in the cracks of the everyday world. As readers, we are compelled to face these terrors, and in doing so, we learn something profound about ourselves: that even when fiction blurs into reality, we have the strength to turn the page and keep going.

Horror's ability to stretch our imaginations, toy with our sense of reality, and challenge our deepest fears is what keeps us coming back. It's not just about the scares—it's about the journey into the unknown, and the thrill of emerging from the darkness, heart racing, but ultimately unscathed.

Chapter 6

Using Psychology to Enhance Storytelling

Horror is at its most powerful when it doesn't just frighten—but gets under the reader's skin. By understanding the psychological mechanisms that drive fear, tension, and emotional investment, writers can craft stories that resonate on a much deeper level. This chapter explores how to use key psychological principles to manipulate pacing, build dread, and shape reader expectations. Whether it's knowing what triggers fear or how the human brain processes suspense, these tools can help you sharpen your narrative edge and deliver horror that truly lingers.

Understanding Your Audience

Crafting a successful horror story involves more than just spooky settings and terrifying monsters. It requires an understanding of human psychology and how different individuals react to fear. Horror writers can leverage psychological principles to deepen the emotional impact of their stories by appealing to specific fear triggers and managing the emotional pacing throughout the narrative.

Every audience has particular fears based on their personal experiences, cultural background, and psychological makeup. Common fear triggers—like the fear of death, the unknown, isolation, or loss of control—are universal across many audiences, but knowing how to appeal to those fears in a targeted way enhances the effectiveness of the story. For example, Alfred Hitchcock was a master at emotional pacing in his films, using tension to keep audiences on edge while offering brief moments of relief (with humor most often), only to heighten the tension again later. This same technique can be applied in horror fiction by carefully orchestrating the emotional highs and lows of a story.

Building tension is another crucial element in horror writing. A sense of growing dread keeps readers hooked, anticipating what might come next. As tension mounts, readers are drawn deeper into the story, and their emotional investment in the characters grows. This emotional engagement makes the eventual horror far more impactful when the fear comes to fruition. Understanding these basic psychological dynamics enables authors to craft a narrative that resonates with their audience on an instinctive level, ensuring the fear lingers even after the book is closed.

Manipulating Fear Responses

The ability to evoke dread, terror, and shock in readers is the cornerstone of effective horror storytelling. By understanding how the brain processes fear, writers can create scenes that tap into the primal fear responses of their audience. The brain's reaction to fear involves a cascade of biochemical reactions, including the release of adrenaline and the activation of the fight-or-flight response. When these fear responses are triggered by a well-crafted scene, readers experience a heightened emotional state that mirrors the characters' own terror.

One powerful technique for manipulating fear responses is through the careful use of dread. Dread is different from shock or terror in that it is a slow, creeping sense of unease that builds over time. Readers are aware that something is wrong, but the exact nature of the threat remains unclear, leaving them in a state of suspense. This gradual build-up can be seen in films like *The Shining* or *Hereditary*, where the horror slowly takes shape, never rushing the revelation of the true terror. By using subtle foreshadowing, unsettling descriptions, and ambiguous situations, writers can effectively instill dread in their readers.

In contrast, terror is often sudden and overwhelming, inducing a visceral fear response. Jump scares in movies often create this feeling, but in literature, terror can be triggered by unexpected plot twists, shocking reveals, or sudden acts of violence. However, these moments need to be used sparingly, as over-reliance on shock can numb readers to fear. To balance this, horror authors can alternate between slow-building dread and sharp moments of terror, keeping readers on their toes.

Psychological horror, which often distinguishes itself from more supernatural or gore-driven sub-genres, taps into internal fears and anxieties. This type of horror doesn't always rely on external threats, like monsters or serial killers, but instead focuses on the psychological breakdown of the characters. Stories like Henry James' *The Turn of the Screw* or Shirley Jackson's *We Have Always Lived in the Castle* derive their terror from paranoia, mental instability, and the fear of the self. These stories manipulate the reader's fear by making them question the reliability of the narrator or the sanity of the characters, leading to a more complex, unnerving experience.

By understanding how fear manifests in the brain and the various emotional and psychological responses it evokes, authors can manipulate these reactions to create horror that sticks with readers long after they've finished the story. Using a combination of dread, terror, and psychological tension, horror writers can craft stories that tap into both primal fears and deeper, more personal anxieties.

1. **Create Relatable Fears:** Horror is most effective when readers *see themselves* in the characters' struggles. Instead of generic "fear of death," dig into personal, specific fears—losing a child, being trapped, having your mind or body taken over. Personalizing fear makes it hit harder.

2. **Use Slow-Building Dread:** Fear doesn't have to come from jump

scares—it's often more effective when it creeps in gradually. Build an atmosphere of unease with small, unsettling details before unleashing the horror. Think of how *Hereditary* slowly unravels into chaos rather than starting with outright terror.

3. **Play With Perception:** Psychological horror thrives on uncertainty. Is your protagonist actually seeing a ghost, or are they losing their mind? Is the town they just entered cursed, or are they succumbing to paranoia? Keeping readers questioning reality makes them more engaged.

4. **Make the Horror Personal:** The best horror isn't just about external monsters—it's about *internal* ones too. Psychological horror often taps into guilt, grief, trauma, or suppressed memories. If your protagonist is battling a literal demon, also make them battle an emotional one.

5. **Let the Fear Linger:** A good horror story doesn't just scare in the moment—it sticks with the reader. Endings that leave some ambiguity, suggest ongoing danger, or force the reader to question reality can make the story more haunting.

Bringing It All Together

Horror fiction isn't just about what scares us—it's about *why* we're scared and *how* that fear shapes our experience. By understanding the psychology of fear, you can craft horror stories that go beyond the surface, burrowing into the minds of your readers and staying with them long after the final page.

Using known psychological Triggers

To heighten emotional impact and maximize fear, horror writers often draw on established psychological triggers—stimuli that consistently evoke strong emotional responses in readers. These are deeply ingrained fears or discomforts that transcend personal experience and tap into universal anxieties.

Common psychological triggers include:

- **Fear of the unknown:** Darkness, isolation, or ambiguous threats can make readers uneasy by denying them clarity or safety. Think of the eerie quiet in *The Blair Witch Project* or the unseen presence in *The Haunting of Hill House*.

- **Loss of autonomy:** Stories involving possession, mind control, or paralysis (like in *Get Out*) play on the fear of losing control over one's own body or will.

- **Contamination and disease:** Used effectively in stories like *The Stand* or *Contagion*, these triggers tap into primal fears of decay, illness, and the breakdown of the body.

- **Vulnerability and helplessness:** Situations where characters are trapped, hunted, or overwhelmed remind readers of their own fragility. This can be emotional (as in *Hereditary*) or physical (like the claustrophobic horror of *The Descent*).

- **Betrayal by Loved Ones:** When someone the protagonist trusts turns out to be the threat (or enables it), it shakes a reader's sense of safety in relationships. This plays out chillingly in *Rosemary's Baby*, where Rosemary's husband conspires against her. It also ties into attachment issues and fear of emotional vulnerability.

- **Fear of Insanity / Losing One's Mind:** The slow descent into madness—or the inability to distinguish reality from delusion—is a powerful trigger. It taps into fears of losing cognitive control. Stories like *The Yellow Wallpaper, Black Swan*, or *Jacob's Ladder* play on this unsettling mental unmooring.

- **The Grotesque / Body Horror:** Distorted or mutilated bodies, unnatural transformations, or loss of bodily integrity trigger deep discomfort, especially when the changes are inflicted upon the self. Think of Cronenberg's *The Fly*, or the gradual transformation in *Annihilation*. This reflects fears of mortality and physical vulnerability.

- **Isolation from Society:** Whether it's physical (like being lost in the wilderness) or social (being ostracized or misunderstood), isolation evokes primal anxieties. Stories like *The Thing, The Shining*, or *I Am Legend* explore how isolation amplifies fear and suspicion.

- **Parental Failure / Harm to Children:** For many readers, anything involving harm to children—or the inability to protect them—strikes a deeply emotional nerve. *Pet Sematary* and *The Babadook* are strong examples. These stories trigger protective instincts and guilt around perceived failure.

- **Inescapable Fate / Loss of Agency:** The feeling that no matter what a character does, doom is inevitable (as in *Final Destination* or *The Ring*) speaks to a fear of powerlessness and existential dread. This often ties in with cosmic horror, where the universe itself is indifferent or hostile.

- **Religious or Moral Corruption:** Possession stories like *The Exorcist*, or tales involving evil clergy or perverted morality, tap into deeply ingrained belief systems. Challenging a reader's spiritual or ethical framework can create profound unease.

- **Identity Erosion / Doppelgängers:** Characters who are replaced, duplicated, or no longer recognize themselves (as in *Invasion of the Body Snatchers* or *Us*) challenge the very concept of self. These stories explore fears of conformity, loss of identity, or being "taken over."

When using psychological triggers, subtlety often works better than shock. Let discomfort simmer beneath the surface before revealing the full threat. And remember, not every fear needs to be monstrous—sometimes the most terrifying horrors are the ones that feel all too human.

Internal vs. External Conflict in Horror

Horror fiction thrives when it balances external threats with internal struggles. While external conflict involves tangible dangers—a killer, a demon, a haunted house—internal conflict dives into the psychological battles within the character. The most memorable horror often fuses both.

External conflict drives the plot. It gives readers a clear antagonist or danger to fear. Think of *Alien*—the creature is the obvious threat. But it's *Ripley's* resilience and moral dilemmas that keep us emotionally engaged.

Internal conflict, on the other hand, elevates the narrative. It explores fear, guilt, grief, denial, or trauma. In *The Babadook*, for example, the monster represents the mother's unresolved grief. The true horror isn't just the creature—it's the emotional breakdown threatening her relationship with her child.

Great horror stories often ask: *What's scarier—the monster outside the door, or the one inside our mind?*

When writers build both layers of conflict, they deepen the emotional impact. Readers aren't just scared for the character's life—they're scared for their soul.

Chapter 7

Horror as a Shared Experience

While horror often feels intimate—something we experience alone in the dark with a book or a film—it's also deeply communal. Fear, after all, is one of the most universal emotions, and horror has a unique way of bringing people together through that shared emotional intensity. Whether it's through discussing terrifying scenes, attending conventions, or bonding over the same stories that haunted our childhoods, horror builds connections.

In this chapter, we'll explore how horror fiction not only reflects cultural memory but also forges strong communities of fans and creators. We'll also examine the role horror plays in helping readers process personal and collective trauma—not in isolation, but side by side with others who find comfort, empowerment, and meaning in the macabre.

Horror as a Shared Cultural Memory

Horror fiction doesn't just scare us—it weaves itself into the fabric of our collective cultural memory. Certain horror stories become more than just terrifying tales; they transform into shared experiences, shaping how entire generations understand and process fear. When someone references *Pennywise the Clown*, *Frankenstein's Monster*, or *The Blair Witch*, there is an immediate recognition, a shared understanding built through years of storytelling, film adaptations, and cultural discourse.

These iconic horror stories act as cultural touchstones, influencing not only literature and film but also the way we talk about fear in everyday life. *Dracula*, for instance, didn't just popularize vampire fiction—it fundamentally shaped Western perceptions of vampires, creating a blueprint that has since evolved but remains recognizable. Similarly, *The Exorcist* reinforced the idea of demonic possession as one of horror's most terrifying and enduring themes, with its influence still visible in modern horror films and literature.

Beyond individual stories, horror as a genre reflects and preserves historical anxieties, becoming a time capsule of the fears of different eras. The *nuclear horror* of the 1950s, embodied in films like *Godzilla* and *Them!*, captured Cold War anxieties about atomic devastation. The *slasher boom* of the 1980s mirrored rising fears about crime and violence in suburban America, while the *found footage horror* of the early 2000s, exemplified by *The Blair Witch Project* and *Paranormal Activity*, played into a generation's growing paranoia about surveillance, reality distortion, and the rise of digital culture.

This collective memory isn't just passive—it's active and evolving. Each new wave of horror builds upon what came before, sometimes paying homage, sometimes subverting expectations. When Jordan Peele's *Us* and *Get Out* were released, audiences didn't just react to them as standalone films—they understood them within the context of horror history, seeing the ways they reinterpreted tropes and themes from classic horror stories.

Horror's ability to ingrain itself into shared memory makes it more than just a genre—it becomes a communal experience. The stories we tell today shape the nightmares of tomorrow, ensuring that horror remains a living, breathing entity that evolves alongside our fears. It is not just something we consume, but something we inherit, pass down, and reinterpret, ensuring that its impact is felt across generations.

Horror Conventions and the Fan Community

Horror is one of the most passionate and dedicated fandoms in the world, and nowhere is that more evident than at horror conventions, fan clubs, and meetups. These events aren't just about celebrating the latest films, books, or collectibles—they're about forging real connections with like-minded people who share a love for the genre. Writers, filmmakers, artists, and fans gather to revel in their collective appreciation for horror, discussing trends, dissecting themes, and introducing one another to new and classic works.

At conventions like *HorrorHound Weekend*, *Monsterpalooza*, or *Texas Frightmare Weekend*, horror fans get to meet their favorite authors and actors, attend panels on the craft of horror storytelling, and explore the artistry behind the genre. There's a thrill in standing shoulder-to-shoulder with others who love *The Texas Chainsaw Massacre*, *The Haunting of Hill House*, or the psychological horrors of *Hereditary* as much as you do. These spaces offer validation, camaraderie, and a reminder that horror is not an isolated experience—it's a thriving, communal one.

Beyond conventions, horror fan clubs and online communities serve as year-round gathering places. From Facebook groups to Reddit threads and Discord servers, fans constantly exchange theories, discuss the scariest scenes they've encountered, and support independent horror creators. The genre has always been a space for outsiders, misfits, and creative thinkers, and in these communities, horror lovers find their people.

Community and Shared Experiences in Horror Fiction

Horror fiction has always been more than just a solitary experience. While reading a horror story alone can be an intensely immersive and chilling experience, horror is often at its most powerful when shared with others. Fear, much like laughter, has a contagious quality. There's something uniquely thrilling about jumping in fright alongside a friend during a horror movie or exchanging ghost stories late into the night, hanging onto every eerie detail.

From the earliest days of oral storytelling, horror has thrived in communal settings. Ancient tribes would gather around fires, passing down tales meant to instill both fear and wisdom. These stories, often about supernatural beings, vengeful spirits, or the dangers lurking in the darkness, were not only entertainment but also a survival tool. They warned listeners of real dangers—both natural and human—while reinforcing the idea that fear was something best faced together.

Today, this tradition continues in various forms, from horror conventions and themed events to book clubs and online discussions. The genre has evolved into a social phenomenon, where fans gather to share their experiences and interpretations. Whether it's through discussing a particularly unsettling scene in a novel, analyzing the subtext of a horror film, or debating the scariest urban legends, horror fosters a sense of camaraderie. Readers and viewers bond over their shared love for the genre, forming communities centered around fear and fascination.

The internet has revolutionized how horror is consumed and discussed, creating vast online spaces where fans can interact, share, and even collaborate on horror storytelling. Online forums, social media groups, Reddit threads, and YouTube analysis videos allow horror enthusiasts to connect in ways that were never possible before. Dedicated horror podcasts dissect the deeper meanings behind beloved classics and introduce fans to hidden gems, while interactive storytelling platforms let users contribute to ongoing horror narratives.

This sense of collective participation intensifies the horror experience. Take the rise of *creepypasta*—digital folklore that has birthed legends like *Slender Man* and *The Backrooms*. These modern horror myths originated in online spaces, where different users added their own interpretations, expanding and evolving the lore. The fear wasn't just in reading these stories—it was in witnessing their growth, knowing that they were shaped by a collective consciousness of horror lovers around the world.

Streaming services and watch parties have also made it easier than ever for horror fans to experience fear together, even from different locations. A shared viewing of a horror movie, whether in a theater or through a virtual watch party, becomes a social event—one filled with screams, nervous laughter, and the occasional "Don't go in there!" shouted at the screen. The power of these experiences reinforces that horror is not just about individual fear but about the thrill of fear shared.

Something fascinating happens when horror is experienced as a group—it becomes more bearable. The presence of others can lessen the intensity of fear, allowing audiences to engage with horror in a way that feels thrilling rather than overwhelming. Neuroscientists have suggested that when we experience fear collectively, our brains process it differently. The emotional response is softened by the comfort of knowing that others are feeling the same thing.

This is why horror movies in a packed theater are often filled with nervous laughter, gasps, and even applause. The tension builds, but the shared reactions offer a kind of emotional release, making the horror more enjoyable rather than deeply distressing. It's the same reason why telling ghost stories at a campfire is exciting—the shared suspense and anticipation make the experience even more electrifying.

Even horror literature, which is typically a solitary medium, finds ways to foster community. Book clubs dedicated to horror fiction thrive because of the discussions that follow a terrifying read. Readers come together to analyze what scared them, what themes resonated, and what twists took them by surprise. These conversations add another layer of engagement to horror storytelling, making it clear that the genre isn't just about fear—it's about connection.

When horror is shared, it isn't just about entertainment—it becomes cathartic. Many horror fans report feeling a sense of relief or emotional cleansing after engaging with terrifying stories. Facing fear together, even in fictional form, can create a feeling of solidarity. It reminds us that fear is universal, something we all experience, and something that ultimately brings us closer.

In this way, horror is a paradox. It isolates characters in terrifying situations but unites its audience through shared experience. It plunges us into fear but ultimately reminds us that we are not alone in our anxieties. Horror fiction, in all its chilling forms, thrives on community—on the retelling, the analysis, and the collective embrace of the dark.

Whether it's through in-person gatherings, online discussions, or the shared thrill of watching a scary movie with friends, horror connects us in ways few other genres can. It turns fear into a social experience, transforming solitary shivers into collective excitement. And that's what keeps us coming back—because while horror may scare us, it also unites us, reminding us that fear is a universal language best spoken together.

Conclusion

The Enduring Power of Horror

Horror fiction has long held a unique place in human culture and psychology. Its endurance can be attributed to its ability to tap into primal emotions and fears that transcend time and place. Horror allows us to confront the unknown, the taboo, and the terrifying—while providing a safe space to explore these emotions. From ancient mythologies to modern-day literature and films, horror persists because it speaks to the darkest parts of the human psyche. Whether exploring the fear of death, the monstrous other, or the fragility of civilization, horror addresses universal themes that resonate with our most basic instincts.

On a personal level, horror offers readers a way to face their fears, release pent-up emotions, and ultimately find catharsis. It acts as a mirror to society's evolving anxieties, allowing both writers and readers to grapple with contemporary issues through a distorted, yet often revealing, lens. Horror remains relevant because it helps individuals and societies make sense of the chaotic and often frightening world around them.

The Future of Horror Fiction:

As society and technology evolve, so too will the fears and anxieties that shape our collective consciousness. The future of horror fiction may explore themes like artificial intelligence, climate disaster, and the erasure of personal identity in an increasingly digital world. Psychological horror, already a dominant sub-genre, will likely continue to grow as we explore mental health, trauma, and isolation in more nuanced ways. The genre may also address the widening gap between reality and virtual experiences, using horror as a way to explore the blurring of these boundaries.

In this evolving landscape, horror fiction will remain vital. Its capacity to adapt and address new fears ensures that it will continue to challenge, terrify, and enlighten, providing readers with the psychological tools to navigate an increasingly complex and unpredictable world. As long as there are fears to confront, horror will persist, helping us understand ourselves and the world around us.

About the author

Joe Mynhardt stands as a paragon in the horror literary world, a Bram Stoker Award-winning South African publisher, editor, author, story coach, and mentor with over a decade of experience. As the founder and CEO of Crystal Lake, Joe has transformed a humble 2012 startup into a multifaceted Intellectual Property powerhouse.

With a track record of working with and publishing works by luminaries such as Clive Barker, Stephen King, Charlaine Harris, Ramsey Campbell, John Connolly, Jack Ketchum, Jonathan Maberry, Christopher Golden, Graham Masterton, Damien Angelica Walters, Adam Nevill, Lisa Morton, Elizabeth Massie, Joe R. Lansdale, Edward Lee, Paul Tremblay, and Wes Craven, Joe is the quintessential mentor for aspiring authors. His deep industry insights and extensive network place him in a unique position to guide both new and seasoned writers in the genre.

Joe is also the author of the Shadows & Ink series, a guide to horror writing and publishing.

Joe's commitment to nurturing talent and fostering author careers is at the heart of Crystal Lake Publishing's ethos. His approach is not just about publishing books; it's about building a community, sharing knowledge, and being a beacon of friendship and guidance in the often-intimidating world of horror writing.

Since leaving his day job in 2016 to focus full-time on his passion, Joe has also excelled as a work-from-home dad, a role he embraced in 2018. His daughter,

Cayleigh, named after his childhood influences Bruce Lee and Stan Lee, is a testament to his belief in the power of storytelling across all mediums. Joe's love for great narratives extends beyond literature, encompassing comics, games, film, and television, with favorites ranging from Poe, Doyle, and Lovecraft to King, Connolly, and Hill.

Joe Mynhardt isn't just a figure in the horror industry—he's a driving force behind it, leading a successful online business that goes beyond the traditional boundaries of publishing. Joe is also the creator and driving force behind The House of Shadows & Ink on YouTube and TikTok.

Discover more about Joe's journey and Crystal Lake's offerings at www.cry stallakepub.com or connect with him on Facebook or Patreon (includes author tiers and a 7-day free trial), where he continues to inspire and lead the next generation of storytellers.

For more from Joe check out his Linktree page:

THE END?

Not if you want to dive into more of Crystal Lake Publishing's Tales from the Darkest Depths!

Check out our amazing website and online store or download our latest catalog here:

We always have great new projects and content on the website to dive into, as well as a newsletter, behind the scenes options, social media platforms, our own dark fiction shared-world series and our very own webstore. Our webstore even has categories specifically for KU books, non-fiction, anthologies, and of course more novels and novellas.

Joe's Shadows & Ink
YouTube channel

Readers...

Thank you for reading *Shadows & Ink Vol.3*. We hope you enjoyed this on writing guide.

If you have a moment, please review *Shadows & Ink Vol.3* at the store where you bought it.

Help other readers by telling them why you enjoyed this book. No need to write an in-depth discussion. Even a single sentence will be greatly appreciated. Reviews go a long way to helping a book sell, and is great for an author's career. It'll also help us to continue publishing quality books.

Thank you again for taking the time to journey with Crystal Lake Publishing.

You will find links to all our social media platforms on our Linktree page.
https://linktr.ee/CrystalLakePublishing

Follow us on Amazon:

MISSION STATEMENT

Since its founding in August 2012, Crystal Lake has quickly become one of the world's leading publishers of Dark Fiction and Horror books. In 2023, Crystal Lake officially transitioned into an entertainment company, joining several other divisions, genres, and imprints, including Torrid Waters, Crystal Lake Comics, Crystal Lake Games, Crystal Lake Kids, and many more.

While we strive to present only the highest quality fiction and entertainment, we also endeavour to support authors along their writing journey. We offer our time and experience in non-fiction projects, as well as author mentoring and services, at competitive prices.

With several Bram Stoker Award wins and many other wins and nominations (including the HWA's Specialty Press Award), Crystal Lake Publishing puts integrity, honor, and respect at the forefront of our publishing operations.

We strive for each book and outreach program we spearhead to not only entertain and touch or comment on issues that affect our readers, but also to strengthen and support the Dark Fiction field and its authors.

Not only do we find and publish authors we believe are destined for greatness, but we strive to work with men and women who endeavour to be decent human beings who care more for others than themselves, while still being hard working, driven, and passionate artists and storytellers.

Crystal Lake Publishing is and will always be a beacon of what passion and dedication, combined with overwhelming teamwork and respect, can accomplish. We endeavour to know each and every one of our readers, while building personal relationships with our authors, reviewers, bloggers, podcasters, bookstores, and libraries.

We will be as trustworthy, forthright, and transparent as any business can be, while also keeping most of the headaches away from our authors, since it's our job to solve the problems so they can stay in a creative mind. Which of course also means paying our authors.

We do not just publish books, we present to you worlds within your world, doors within your mind, from talented authors who sacrifice so much for a moment of your time.

There are some amazing small presses out there, and through collaboration and open forums we will continue to support other presses in the goal of helping authors and showing the world what quality small presses are capable of accomplishing. No one wins when a small press goes down, so we will always be there to support hardworking, legitimate presses and their authors. We don't see Crystal Lake as the best press out there, but we will always strive to be the best, strive to be the most interactive and grateful, and even blessed press around. No matter what happens over time, we will also take our mission very seriously while appreciating where we are and enjoying the journey.

What do we offer our authors that they can't do for themselves through self-publishing?

We are big supporters of self-publishing (especially hybrid publishing), if done with care, patience, and planning. However, not every author has the time or inclination to do market research, advertise, and set up book launch strategies. Although a lot of authors are successful in doing it all, strong small presses will always be there for the authors who just want to do what they do best: write.

What we offer is experience, industry knowledge, contacts and trust built up over years. And due to our strong brand and trusting fanbase, every Crystal Lake Publishing book comes with weight of respect. In time our fans begin to trust our judgment and will try a new author purely based on our support of said author.

With each launch we strive to fine-tune our approach, learn from our mistakes, and increase our reach. We continue to assure our authors that we're here for them and that we'll carry the weight of the launch and dealing with third parties while they focus on their strengths—be it writing, interviews, blogs, signings, etc.

We also offer several mentoring packages to authors that include knowledge and skills they can use in both traditional and self-publishing endeavours.

We look forward to launching many new careers.

This is what we believe in. What we stand for. This will be our legacy.

Welcome to Crystal Lake Publishing—Where Stories Come Alive!